WHETSTONE

BOOKS BY LORNA CROZIER

POETRY
Inside Is the Sky (1976)
Crow's Black Joy (1979)
Humans and Other Beasts (1980)
No Longer Two People (with Patrick Lane) (1981)
The Weather (1983)
The Garden Going On Without Us (1985)
Angels of Flesh, Angels of Silence (1988)
Inventing the Hawk (1992)
Everything Arrives at the Light (1995)
A Saving Grace (1996)
What the Living Won't Let Go (1999)
Apocrypha of Light (2002)
Bones in Their Wings: Ghazals (2003)
Whetstone (2005)

ANTHOLOGIES
A Sudden Radiance (with Gary Hyland) (1987)
Breathing Fire (with Patrick Lane) (1995)
Desire in Seven Voices (2000)
Addicted: Notes from the Belly of the Beast
(with Patrick Lane) (2001)
Breathing Fire 2 (with Patrick Lane) (2004)

WHETSTONE

LORNA CROZIER

Library and Archives Canada Cataloguing in Publication

Crozier, Lorna, 1948-
Whetstone / Lorna Crozier.

Poems.
ISBN 0-7710-2467-3

I. Title.

PS8555.R72W47 2005   C811'.54   C2004-905954-8

We acknowledge the financial support of the Government of Canada through the Book Publishing Industry Development Program and that of the Government of Ontario through the Ontario Media Development Corporation's Ontario Book Initiative. We further acknowledge the support of the Canada Council for the Arts and the Ontario Arts Council for our publishing program.

The epigraph on page vii is an excerpt from *The Great Fire* by Shirley Hazzard. Copyright © 2003 by Shirley Hazzard. Reprinted by permission of Farrar, Straus and Giroux, LLC.
The epigraph to "The Physics of the Rose" on page 24 is from *God's Equation* by Amir D. Aczel.

Typeset in Garamond by M&S, Toronto
Printed and bound in Canada

This book is printed on acid-free paper that is 100% recycled, ancient-forest friendly (100% post-consumer recycled).

McClelland & Stewart Ltd.
The Canadian Publishers
481 University Avenue
Toronto, Ontario
M5G 2E9
www.mcclelland.com

1 2 3 4 5   09 08 07 06 05

For my mother and for Patrick

"I realise, too, that I now have a substantial past – which means that I am no longer young but have become more interesting to myself."

– Shirley Hazzard, *The Great Fire*

CONTENTS

WHETSTONE

AUTOBIOGRAPHY: BIRTH

In my old bones I make the journey back.
My mother's mother has come in from the farm,
my brother waits at the table for our father
who didn't believe I'd arrive today;
he's betting on the horses – *Tony, Prophet,*
Sweet Forgetting – at the Gull Lake Fair.
At seven, my brother knows what he can do,
his new knife cutting through caragana,
how he can strip the fibre to the wood's white heart
and leave us all behind, that glint in his pocket.

I drop my bones in the kindling box
and then I'm out the window, high and fast
to where breath flutters in the lilac leaves
and all the deaths I'm heir to
turn a little from their tasks and look at me.
There's so much light beneath the moon,
my shadow's there below
as if some part of me has fallen:
a stain where a hand has rested
on skin that holds a bruise.

With all this sky to cross
how can Jesus find you? Surely
there's too much of it, even for one
who's called the Lord of Light. You try to find
the stone that speaks in tongues. The rooster
who's an angel with a useful job.
Sometimes wind leaves its footprints
on the water. Sometimes the dust's
a voice that rises when a car goes past.
A god is walking through the wheat fields,
you're sure of that. But it's not you he's come for.
There are coyotes to save, the wheat itself, short
and shriven, and the skunk who's about to eat
the poisoned egg. Let alone the egg, the song inside it.
The devil seems to have more focus; he believes
you deserve his full attention. If you hang your soul
on the line he's right there, especially if it's pinned
beside a good woman's laundry,
her cotton underwear so thin from all the washings,
light passes through it and is changed.

BEAUTY

It's not the antelope's
              golden leaps across the grasslands
but how she stops

drops to her knees at the barbed-wire fence
                          and crawls under
      then springs when she's on her feet again

So too with you. The beauty's in
     your fall, your startled
             grace —

     everything
        turning on
the hinges of your neck, waist, and knees
                 how you bend —

SAND FROM THE GOBI DESERT

Sand from the Gobi Desert blows across Saskatchewan,
becomes the irritation in an eye. So say the scientists who
separate the smallest pollen from its wings of grit,
identify the origin and name. You have to wonder where
the dust from these fields ends up: Zimbabwe, Fiji,
on the row of shoes outside a mosque in Istanbul,
on the green rise of a belly in the Jade Museum in Angkor Wat?
And what of our breath, grey hair freed from a comb, the torn
    threads of shadows?
Just now the salt from a woman's tears settles finely its invisible kiss
on my upper lip. She's been crying in Paris on the street that means
Middle of the Day though it's night there, and she doesn't want
    the day to come.
Would it comfort her to know another, halfway round the world,
    can taste her grief?
Another would send her, if she could, the rare flakes of snow
falling here before the sunrise, snow that barely fleeces the brown
    back of what's
too dry to be a field of wheat, and winter's almost passed. Snow
    on her lashes.
What of apple blossoms, my father's ashes, small scraps of sadness
that slip out of reach? Is it comforting to know the wind
never travels empty? A sparrow in the Alhambra's arabesques
rides the laughter spilling from our kitchen, the smell of garlic
makes the dust delicious where and where it falls.

CALM

The lake has gone beyond reason. It drifts out of itself,
casts shadows and reflections across the skirts of fir

greening the shore, making of their wind-still study
a flicker and slide, the way souls must move, ichorous, transparent,

hovering near the flesh before they go. I want the green under
    green,
the thought below the thought, the one deep down and cold,

ravelling its divination in the dark. Are there gods who need
no slaking? Ungathered, the water's blank and beautiful,

intricately wrought. No one knows where mind and body
come together, that clean join fingerlings slip through.

WHEN MY FATHER LIVED ON EARTH

The second time my father lived on earth
he was my father. There were many things
he did and didn't do. Out of them he made
a storm and salt. Hands that held my head
when it was small and wet.
The first time? I want him to have been
something I could've seen or touched,
red osier in the coulee's cleft,
a hare halfway to being winter.
I want him to have been fresh snow
scooped into a basin and set
on the south side of the house to melt
so a man could wash the shirt he'd wear
to meet his lover. Once he was thin air,
an iron hasp, an opening. Storm and salt
were what my father left me.
The many things he did and didn't do.

LEAVING HOME

When Louis Armstrong left New Orleans for Chicago
at King Oliver's request, his mother
packed him a trout sandwich and no one met him
at the train, though he could blow his trumpet
and be heard across state lines. I don't know why,
but I love to think of that trout sandwich he carried
in his pocket and later ate, the wheels spinning him
into fame, though it took some years and at least
two women. When my dad and I went fishing
Mom laid roast chicken from the day before
between slices of store-bought white. Was there mayonnaise?
I don't remember, but in the boat, a few fish biting,
our fingers shone with butter as if we'd dipped our hands in fire
then treated them for burns. The sun was bright but weaker,
the afternoons so long I watched the hairs on my father's arms
turn gold. If I'd been called away by someone other than myself,
years later, that's what I'd have wanted, chicken on white bread,
and the thing that turned my breath and body into music.
Leaving home like Louis Armstrong – though there's no one like
    him –
and his trumpet. And the sandwich he saved until he reached
the outskirts of Chicago, savouring the Southern taste of what
his mother made him. Imagine those fingers, that mouth.

SOMETHING ELSE

Belly-snug on the floor, linoleum
warmed by the woodstove, I watched
the tongue of our new pup lapping milk.
Red as a fox, she fit into my mother's hand.

I told my friends she'd come from far away
by train, told them my father claimed her
at the station in a wooden box like the ones
full of oranges from Japan. Just last year
Mom said I'd got it wrong. She came from
Mrs. Rittinger on Sixth, we lived on Fourth.
Those days, Dad drove an oil-delivery truck.
Behind his boss's back, he'd swapped a good month's
worth of heat for a purebred Pomeranian.

Though she became my brother's dog
she slept with me because he tossed
too much in sleep. When she was older
if I moved at all, she'd growl and nip.
I learned to lie like a statue on a tomb,
carnelian dog on a marble cushion at my feet.

One morning from the neighbour's porch
I saw her skulk past our kindling stack
and with her teeth turn the wooden latch
on the cage Dad had built to hold two ducklings
he'd won tossing coins at the summer fair.

He was always winning things like that –
a guinea pig named Elvis, a one-winged turkey,
those golden ducks I loved.

From a distance I couldn't cross,
I watched her disappear into the cage
then back right out, her muzzle bloody.
She made no sound, just closed the latch –
she was that smart – then trotted off between the lilacs.
Mom said later the dog was jealous;
the ducks had trailed my brother everywhere
as I did if he'd let me.

When my brother left for good, she was mine
as much as anyone's. For a time she followed me
as if I'd take her to him. I didn't know where
he'd gone, just far away, too far for him
to write or visit. Things changed
then. Everything got older fast.

The day my father put that small red pup
beside the kitchen stove,
my mother named her Tiny.
I would have called her something else.

WINTER BIRCHES

Even the ground needs rest.
Frozen eight feet down, it won't
take the dead any more. The few
who will not wait till spring
are pulled on sleds across the snow
to the birch grove north of town.

There, they turn that white, that
ghostly. They'll sometimes step
toward you in the moonlight,
arms outstretched or reaching up,
mouths stuffed with snow.

When that happens it's best
to keep on walking. Pretend
you never knew them,
your own face cold.
It's winter, after all. It's night.

If you hear your name
don't look back. Think of water
running under ice, a green bud opening.
Say they're only birch trees,
they're only trees. Don't
think of what that means.

PRAYERS OF SNOW

Snow is a lesson in forgetting, a lesson in gravity,
a long loose sentence spiralling to the end of thought.
It prays to the young god robed in white, his ascent
a blizzard returning to the sky. It prays to the white-footed
mouse, the snowy owl, the varying hare and vole,
the cat with fur between his toes. It closes the gap
between drought and plenty, belief and blasphemy,
the ear and silence. It is a migration of birds
without eyes, without feet, who settle white in branches
on breasts and wings. When you stride through snow
in dreams or waking, you are a star-walker.
It prays to the soft fall of your boots.

THE SIMPLEST OF MOVEMENTS

The Noh actor, rehearsing for a play in London,
couldn't make the simplest of movements.
Such as, sitting in a chair and lighting a cigarette.
Such as, cutting a loaf of bread while talking
over his shoulder to an imaginary wife.
Then the director said, *Show me Ariel.*
The others in the cast stayed
in their feet and thighs while he
made instantly of his body a lightness
that flitted and swooped through the wings
though he stood –
what we would have called –
perfectly still.

WHETSTONE

The stone that sharpens stars,
      their slow slice across the sky.
Flat, black, and shot with mica. For twenty years

it must have mingled with the gravel
          on the road I run. Now its light
has reached my eyes.

What does it want from me?
      To be moved into another
galaxy of knives? To be looked upon and left

where it has found me? Maybe it's just a stone
      among other stones, desireless
and unafflicted.

The only colour black can be
      yet it is star-sparked, sun-salted.
Does it know I am

dulled by God?
      His negligence,
          his under-use.

THREE MOVEMENTS FOR THE WIND

Without a mother, without a father,
wind carries no resemblance anywhere it goes.

One barb on the wire catches a tuft of wind.
This is the only thing that happens for miles.

Chime, sock, mill, flower: hook a word
to the wind and it will move.

WHAT COMES AFTER

I am my own big dog.
Walk, and I'm at the door,
eat, and I take what I offer,
lie down, and I curl on the floor,
my heavy head between my paws.

I don't need anything but this,
I don't think of what comes after.

I sing the way a dog sings,
I weep the way a dog weeps.
Every night at my feet
I am a big sack of sleep
stinking of me.

DROUGHT

Water is suddenly old.
It feels a stiffness,
a lessening deep down.

Now if you row past the reeds,
drop a bucket on a rope
and pull it up,

water won't have
the strength to turn
that darkness into light.

THE LIGHT IN MY MOTHER'S KITCHEN

Three green tomatoes on the windowsill,
offerings the household gods will not refuse.
My mother isn't here, but the bulb glows
in the small house of the oven
where something firm and golden
pushes against the tin walls of a pan.
If my father were alive he'd be asking
What's for supper? He'd be sitting
at the table with a beer and cigarette,
his hard heels on the rung of a chair,
my mother with her back to him,
as if he'd spoken out of turn,
as if he'd asked too much again.
The smell of yeast, and no one talking.
The sound of the fridge saving everything
that can be saved. As the sun disappears
the oven casts its light on what will feed us.
Cigarette smoke rises, the dark breath
of my father filling my mouth.

TO SEE CLEARLY

> "See how many ends this stick has!"
> – Montaigne

The strawlike strands of grass are frosted
only on one side, but the thorn
of the wild rose is feathered all around,
even on its tip, a soft flared tuft.

The task: to see clearly
so that even the ear becomes a kind of eye
taking you beyond the small circle
of your sight – even the mouth –
magpie, magpie over the southern hill.

In the grove, birches move in and out of snow
as if the wind were made of wheels and pulleys,
trees dropping from the sky so suddenly
you gasp and fog your glasses.

Instead of shadows there are streaks of gold!

Don't think the snow can't see you
reeling in the light.

ICE-FOG

The air annunciates. It breathes a frosty haze
on my pants and jacket as if I'm growing fur.
Immeasurable, indifferent, now it can be touched
and tasted. It can be seen. Have I fallen through
to the other side of morning or risen above clouds?
This weight, this stillness: splendour thickening.
Down the road a dog barks. Someone walks toward me,
head and shoulders plumed with white. Father?
Lord of Winter? O Death! When his lips touch mine
they will be feathers. I don't know what to do.
I pray for wind, for sun, I pray for my father to speak
before he turns to crystals as he turned to ash.
In the visible around me hoarfrost
hallucinates a thousand shards of bone.

DROUGHT

In such a time rain could have anything
it wanted: a roofless house,
days without worry, goatskin gloves
to warm its long grey fingers.

The farmers would even sacrifice
a daughter, one who'd never
seen in seven years
the bare branch blossom.

With a veil of rain, a thread of rain,
she'd walk into rain's labyrinth;
outside her parents' house the trees
turning green with grief.

FORM

The chickadee
drops
to the middle
of the lily pad

makes it dip a little

just enough water
slips over the edge
for the bird
to bathe.

SHADOW

To lie on one side of a tree
then another, over rough or smooth.

To feel cool along one's whole body
lengthening without intent,
nothing getting in the way.

To give up on meaning.
To never wear out or mar.

To move by increments like
a beautiful equation, like the moon
ripening above the golden city.

To be doppelganger,
the soft underside of wings,
the part of cumulus that slides
thin promises of rain across the wheat.

To disappear. To be blue
simply because snow has fallen
and it's the blue hour of the day.

THE SILENCE OF CREATION

After Adam did what he was told
and named the animals,
God created the unnamable.
Lean and sinewy like something old;
a small afterthought, it seemed back then,
the crucial work all done.

But soon the names of things began
to disappear, and then the things themselves,
muteness moving in, slowly at first,
like numbness at the ends of fingers.

Far from the dream that is Eden,
it is hard for us now to believe
in the fluent blooms of Paradise
where the blood of Adam's naming
stepped, finned and fluttered
into the greening of the light.

Was it envy? Was it loneliness –
the no one God could talk to –
that made Him say, "Let there be silence,"
just as the world began to sing?

THE PHYSICS OF THE ROSE

"'The electron,' the professor said, 'lives in a different space from
the one we live in.'"
  – Amir D. Aczel, *God's Equation*

Each petal an eyelid, blood-fused, over what
invisible eyes! How it inhabits *now*,
        how it occupies the whole house of your seeing.
Fold after fold, its silence so enclosed
it seems a kind of speaking, light's muted
                              hallelujah brought inside.

Shocking as a heart cut out and set in glass,
it makes the room spin around it.
                    The antithesis of absence,
of stillness, its red fist unfurling
this, *this* and *this*, a daring to be open
so immoderate you want to say *outrageous*,
you want to say *ridiculous*, but can't.

Clothed or not, you stand naked in its eyes.
            Small and unadorned,
without a lover.

LAZARUS

Said nothing day after day.

The scribes and priests who waited
for something to write down, returned
to their temples, mouths and pockets
empty. But for fear of the messiah,
they would've beaten him with sticks,
they would have burned his tongue
until he spoke in ashes.

Even his two sisters grew sick of him:
that dry cough, his constant weeping,
the way his feet shuffled in the dust
as if he'd never left it.

Revulsion of their flesh, they said,
that's what made him spend the nights
far from the house, alone in the dark.
How could they know it was their hair
that drove him to the fields?

The sound of it growing
in their sleep.

IT IS NIGHT

Wind turns back the sheets of the field.
What needs to sleep, sleeps there.
What needs to rest.

The door has fallen from the moon.
It floats in the slough, all knob and hinges.

Now the moon's so open
anything could walk right through.

Only the fox is travelling.
One minute he's a cat, the next a coyote.

Enough light to see by
yet my mouth lies in darkness.
What needs to sleep, sleeps there.
What needs to rest.

Outside my mind, the wind is reckoning.
Always there is something
to figure out.

ANONYMITY

The country of the dead keeps growing.
Is my father lost there, too? Nameless,
without schooling or belief, our love for him
worn thin. Do the animals he killed remember him?
The horses his neighbours couldn't shoot,
the dog who dragged her sack of guts
studded with gravel from the road to our door.

So many times, outside the house,
I refused to know him.
I'd turn my back on the slant-six Fairlane,
black and white, the muffler he installed
illegal even then, the roar in the street
not a teenage pal, but my Dad.

Now I want him behind the wheel again,
his colour back. Seventy-three and thundering
past the tall white houses of the dead,
louder than their strings and benedictions,
so they'll *have* to notice him, so they'll say out loud,
There he goes, and have to name him:
Emerson Crozier in his souped-up Ford.

RAPTURE

Will Jesus come to the small towns first?
Folks lined up in lawn chairs along the street
as if waiting for a late parade: the Lord in hat
and snakeskin boots on a chestnut mare, or leading
the Lions' band, light around him brighter
than the sun bouncing off the mayor's tuba.

Or will he descend to the city?
Down to the deepest part, the underground
mechanics of moving people from dark to dark
one of his delights, the fervour of getting on
and off, the signs – their good direction.

I want him to come where I am now
among the chickadees on the grid I walk,
small chatty angels lighting on his palms,
black feet singed, or yellow warblers circling
above his head, flicking like sparks
from an old-fashioned Zippo with a flint
that needs replacing.

At the line of washing in the farmyard,
though they've gone electric, the woman
will suddenly drift higher than the sheets,
her arms flapping, the collie wagging
at the awkward, fleshy soul she is,
what never sang before now singing

as the subway six hundred miles east
spills its travellers, no matter what the stop,
onto rising silver stairs and they are lifted
to the glass doors of the burning city, oh,
their blistered eyes.

BRUSHES MADE FROM ANIMAL HAIR

The badger clamped the broken branch
                              between his teeth.
The boy gripped the other end,

afraid to let go, for hours in the field
                    dragged that fierceness
backwards – a step or two

then a standoff   a stutter forward,
back again – the half mile
                    to the shelterbelt around the farm.

This is the pull
                    the painter feels in the brush.

What happened when the boy made it, almost home?
What happened when his arms gave out?
What is the source of light?

FOUR COWS IN MOONLIGHT

Just before the evening milking,
the moon so big and golden,
the cows in the pasture are watching it rise,
two Holsteins standing, two reclining,
udders swung to one side.

On his master's whistle a border collie
switches through the grass
to bring them home. He, too, stopping,
sensing something, looking up.

When I'm near, the cows don't startle
or glance my way. White patches flare
on their foreheads, backs, and hips;
udders flush a deeper pink,
the milk inside them also moonspill.

How can we call cows stupid?
I was the one walking past that brightness,
my mind on lesser things,
until I saw their faces lifted,
their blazed, moon-baffled eyes.

MELANOMA

The sea keeps coming in,
no one talking. I have to
sit down with the word
for a while. The waves

leave nothing here,
just an upper lip
pinched in the sand
at the highest point.
It keeps on changing.

Many-boned
and maculate, my feet,
one with a scar –
that's what I wanted
to come to –
one with a scar
shaped like a willow leaf.

It glows in the absence
of any light, that other tide
– the dark one –
rolling in.

LETTER HOME: TOO MUCH, TOO LITTLE

With autumn's lessening comes
a fullness. When I arrived late summer
only random geese flew above the lake
as if the one who gets them ready
waited for a shipment of new hinges
to make the intricate connection between
the heart and the beating of the wings.
Now, two weeks later, countless flocks cross
the great star-bear, refiguring the constellations.
Soon they'll be beyond my hearing.
The swimmers gone, water makes more noise
because there's nothing to distract it.
A loon does not reply. Too much solitude
has made me thin but I'm getting better
at saying what I mean. Nothing's wasted.
Yesterday the woman who sold me milk
and stamped my letter
placed two fingers over the hole in her throat
so she could speak.

POEM FOR A HARD TIME

Chickens
in a shed with screens to let in air,
a small door for them
to step in and out, not an inch
to spare. All things

in their place, particular,
the proper attention paid
so that around them
there seems a kinder light.

And then the eggs to gather,
one by one, warm in your palm.
Each tiny sun contained,
unbroken, no need for it to rise
or fall, no need for anything
to harm you.

WHAT REFUSES FORM

She can't lie down or sit upright
but reclines in the Lazy-Boy night and day,
feet raised, the tumour at the base of her spine
demanding this in-between, halfway state
though sunlight from the window falls
without cleaving on the wooden floor.

Every time he comes inside he brings in panic
with the cold, on the doormat snow puddling
around his boots. If this were a place of miracles
he could say the boots were weeping;
he could say *immaculate heart.* The pain, too,

is without form or edges. It slurs across her face,
a dark smudge coming from far off, that smell
in the air before rain, but the smell here
is more corporeal, marshlike, smeared
with flickers that sink, divide, and rot.
What good is he? Her silence, her refusal

to be wise makes him awkward, a tourist
without language, bargaining for something
he doesn't want to own. The only thing
he knows is the heaviness around her
he can't split or lighten, the air itself thickening
silently, unseen. Though she cannot ease

his burden, he can sense she's drifting from him.
Beside her chair he feels himself grow smaller
and almost lifts a hand to wave. Pain moves
out from her like a wake across the water –
the sharp liquid V that is also the flight of birds.

SETTING

Light dozes into autumn and late afternoon.
The good dishes clean, the table set.
One place missing a spoon.

The crow's flown off with it.
He's laying his own meal on a black cloth.

Something you can chew on,
something you can spit out,
something you can share

with that part of you
you've given nothing to
all your life.

SOLITUDE

Sometimes the dark's so dark
nothing can move through it.
Even the wind, even the geese
who just an hour ago
charcoaled their journey from star to star.
You love the lake at night
because water keeps its distance
yet carries sound, crackled and clear,
from the farthest shore. Sometimes
the hard notes of a party
drift through the screen from cabins
on the southern spit. You said
nothing moves through this dark.
But music does, and voices,
and you go on.

Ripple after ripple of lake-light
breaks on the sand and stays there.
The faraway has just passed through.
The day is small but it begins with so much
beauty, I am poured out like water.
A red squirrel stands upright on the woodpile,
clenches his paws on his chest and stares,
wanting me to choose. Maybe it was Jesus on the lake
in his fishing boat, the disciples pulling up their nets,
light from their faces and hands – *his* face, *his* hands –
what water carries to the shore, the hard gleam of heaven.
There should be music. Harps in the birches,
psalters and a drum. I dance on the sand,
twirl one way, then the other. The fire begins in my feet.
There should be baskets for the fish, there should be
hunger. That I can give you. I used to shine.

REBUTTAL TO THE HIGHER POWER

Think of all the names the unnamed could borrow –
     blue-eyed, fescue, little quaking –
if it had a mind to.
     You lie down in the pasture,

     the back of your head
pressing into green like a fieldstone
that's stayed in the same place
     since muscles of ice heaved it to the sun.

Beneath you grass stretches its roots
     farther than an arm and hand
can reach into water. They douse for darkness,
draw it up to meet the light, or is it light

the dark becomes on this other side
     where footsteps fall?
Through hollow stems, grass siphons
the can't-be-seen

     and sends it out ignited.
It's what gives the shine to everything
     that roots, inclines, or rises only inches.
Dirt, lichen, stone, their telluric under-glitter.

It's the gloriole of wild oats
in all the ditches, the nodding seedheads.

The same nod as the birch bough's,
the rowboat on its tether,

the same nod –
        no – slightly different
as the crow's, as he hops stiff-kneed around
the roadkill. As if everything but you

knows the body's way of saying *yes*,
all afternoon
        the grass replying
                when the invisible asks.

DROUGHT

Dirt hems your jeans and the long dress
you wore when spring got hitched to summer,
gravel pinging like rice on a Chevy hood, so hot
your hand burns when you touch it.

Someone's nailed a foreclosure sign
on the barley field. You begin to hate
the colour blue even in delphiniums,
even in the slough made bluer by its lips of salt.

So many auctions in the country:
that mad roll of syllables blowing in
from all directions, the heart's true music
plaintive and crude, gone to the man
in the red cap, two bits once,
two bits twice, and sold.

High above the heat, clouds aren't good
for anything but adding up the losses,
carry the one, carry the one,
when you want the one to fall.

HOPING TO FIX UP, A LITTLE, THIS WORLD

The cat we've named Basho
plays with the ghost cat who slips
from bamboo to drink at the pond
when the sun begins to fall.
Our other cat, the shy one, climbs
the slow branches of the pear,
and you, my love, go to bed
again too soon. Too much sun?
I ask. Did you forget to wear your hat?

Dusk gives way to darkness
and leaves behind its watchfulness.
The cats absorb it. They see what I am
missing, what I can't make out.

At the pond I light three candles
and float them on the water.
Fish flare up, combustible as coals;
they warm the lotus bud that swells
to breaking but will not open. How long
your sleeping makes the night.

DRINKING IN MOONLIGHT

"No one to drink with
well, there's the moon."
    – Li Po

Hey, the moon's been hungover
three nights
after drinking with you!

Look at it
lying on its back, pale thing,
the top of its head completely gone!

It's got one foot
on a carpet of clouds
but the earth's still tilting.

Now the tides
won't high and low
when they're supposed to.

Don't raise your jar to coax it down!
Don't sing your tavern songs!

The tree frogs and coyotes
have fallen mute. Cranes
go off in the wrong direction

and in the grass there is no dew
to soak the lovers' clothing –
they pull it on too soon!

TU FU WARNS LI PO WHEN LI PO DEPARTS AFTER A NIGHT OF CAROUSING

Don't fall out of your boat!
On this shallow lake
storms rise up without warning

and the eye that sees double,
that makes the steadfast
wobble and bob

doesn't know
if the light ahead
is from another boat

caught in the worst,
or if it's from a stove
a woman's lit on shore

to fry fish for her husband,
hoping the smell
will lead him home.

WHAT CAN'T BE SEEN

After sunset I walk under spruce boughs,
looking for the owl the others saw midday.
Huge, they said, it took up so much *being*,
so much heartspan in the air. *Whoo, whoo,*
I move toward it, no moon or stars,
my way snow-lit.

Above the branches foxed in blacker
than the sky, I hope to see its ears
in silhouette, the shoulder-shrug of wings.
Whoo, whoo, louder now, then nothing.
It seems just in front of me and high.

Beneath the trees, I stand inside
my many years, inside the owl's
deep hearing – its hush, my hush,
circling out and out and touching
our grey heads. Let this be
the what-I-don't-see I die with,
this feathered, thick-lapped
listening of the night.

AT ANNY'S STABLE

The biggest death
I'd ever seen, anything
that was light, that was wind,
gone out of him.

The vet who put him down
knelt by his side, removed the shoes,
one leg resting on the other,
back and front, and gave them
to the woman who was weeping.

Next morning before the backhoe
I go out again. He's on his back,
mouth twisted, legs straight up
and stiff. Flies jewel
his chestnut head.

Maybe this is where
the legends start, Pegasus
and the Horses of the Sun.
His hooves – unnailed –
run on cumulus and blue, wings
sprouting first above his ankles
where the bones wouldn't mend.

WINTER DAY

All night the stars have fallen. Snow
resurrects their light. In winter you are closer
to heaven though you may not know it.

Clouds lie down in white and silent fields,
undulant, unplanted. Outside, your breath
separates from the air around you,

turns crystal on your brows and lashes,
your lower lip. You lick a sweetness,
the taste of what your body has twice-warmed.

Stand still: you'll hear the hands of the wind
working, without commission,
freeing from the nothingness of snow

the forms it finds along the fenceline,
the ribs of drifts climbing up the ditches,
hollows where deer have rested for the night.

Veined with shadows, the snow's marmoreal.
With a single chisel, wind sculpts your body.
It gives you this one day.

LEAVING THE GARDEN

I don't know why I threw the apple.
The air so thick maybe I thought
it would stall, mid-flight, the rain
that had yet to fall smelling of rust
as if it hung above the orchard in buckets
made from old machines. In the shadow
of the tallest tree there was a stranger,
waiting. Did I throw it to frighten her?
Did I throw it to make her see?
Nothing marked the day
as different, the almanac assured
a gentle rain, no frost or early snow.
Even now I'd do it again, throw it
without remorse and watch her leave the garden,
her mouth stuffed with leaves.
No, the old story can't be told
again, the old song is over.

FAMILY CUSTOM

Just before the woman died
her daughter cut off the buds
of all the tulips in the house.
My friend who works for Hospice
tells me this. Was it ritual, family custom,
personal request? She can't say,
but they were Vietnamese and Buddhist,
and they knew exactly what to do.

No flowers brought the season
into my father's hospital room
though my mother could have snipped
some May blooms from their garden.
A close-up photo of a horse hung by the bed,
his gaze turned to the side. My father's
face was yellow and he could not eat.
Don't you look good today? the ward nurse said.

Though I wasn't in the Buddhist house
I can see the tulips' hard red fists
on a linen cloth beside a milk-glass vase.
In my father's room, waiting was
the only thing we knew to do. For hours
I wondered what the horse was looking at
outside the frame, tried to make him
turn his head, hold this dying in his eyes.

Those scarlet tulips, they didn't know
they wouldn't open; dense and darkening
round the edges, they gleam where
they have fallen. If they'd been cut off
here, I'd have put one in my mouth.

DIVINING

The wind's low listening: how it turns
every leaf beneath the trees, swirls cilia of snow
so the snow hears too the warm earth stirring.

I try to listen in that way, the grace notes
on the underside of sound, what my mother wanted
to say, what my father wished he hadn't,
my brother's teasing, how it makes me
stumble still and think I'll fail.

The horizon was a line we couldn't hear
except when a jet traced it white across the sky
and that was rarer then. I'd know the poplar's
rush and sighs outside my childhood window
anywhere, but it's grown taller or it's gone.
It comes now in a different way
like the almost-sound of falling snow,
or the cry of my first lover.

They say hearing's the last to go. After sight,
taste, the loss of smell and touch, it's the rustle
of someone's hands turning you over in a bed,
dry wind through a screen, death's whisper.

The ear's a diviner, then. It witches sounds
like water from under clay, dipping
its bone-wands deep into the dark.

ALL THINGS PASSING

"Every Friday buries a Thursday if you come to look at it."
   – James Joyce, *Ulysses*

Each new day cloaks itself in mourning –
that's why it begins in darkness.
Friday doesn't know it will be dead
by midnight too, buried with the hours
beneath the western pine. The cows in the south pasture
don't know, come Saturday, they'll be struck by lightning,
all twelve under the tree, their hooves blown off.
Death's barbecue. Funeral meats after rain.
In our garden the camellia's brown before
the blossom's fully open. Designed for that:
samsara's flower, *is, is, is,* it simply says,
unfurling what we know but startling us each time.
The plum's another story: even in the dark
the bees are working, zipping back and forth
between its petals and their waxy tombs.
Remember the honey in the skull, the mind
made out of sweetness? Sunday's come again.
O Lord of Dailyness, give us the common
bread and ease of each lost thing.

COUNTING THE MAGPIE

"Souls of poets dead and gone."
   – Keats

                    Warm-blooded
explosion into air, breath spinning into matter,
                         becoming *bird*, long-tailed
exactness of black and white.

Its feet are tar-walkers, waders into lightlessness
                    precisely deep. How heavy the soul is
in that feathered body! How it loves its weight,

            its magus head conjuring beauty
in spilled blood and carcass, in blowfly scab.
   Death-feeder song-spoiler the stretched-like-sinew

sound you can't make into music – count the magpie,
the soul's raw cry that needs no other's singing:
                         one, and one, and one.

SUMMER SMALL TALK

1. After Rain

Spiders,
rain has given away
your secrets:

little death stars,
little abattoirs
the flies zip past.

2. Insect Invisible to the Eye

In tall grasses
the click-click of small
scissors snipping cloth.

Tailor of the meadow,
how he works
while it's still light.

Out of the blue
dragonflies drop in
with their orders:

something long and straight
without waist or shoulders,
something with a sheen.

3. A Shift in the Light

The piebald peonies
want to leap the fence

want the first *e*
struck from their name

want to rip the grass
without remorse.

You'll have to be wary,
never carry secateurs or bit;

approach them with a smile
and an apple in your hand,

their big teeth flashing.

4. Karl Marx Observes the Flowers

Bees without
picks and pit lamps
crawl backwards
from the perfumed
shafts, their miners'
faces dusted gold.

LATE JULY

The crow knows what's going to happen
to everyone. Made large by death,
the sky's more watchful than before.
Someone opens a window. Does a bird
fly out? A boy stands among the lilac bushes,
too late for blooms. All his mother had
of beauty, their scent sickened the rooms.
If he doesn't move, nothing worse will happen.
His mind frightens him. It's like an axe falling
on the chopping block, heat thickening
with blood, the crow flying headless
in small arcs across the yard.

The exhaustion of flowers, midafternoon,
the stale sun's spill and stutter
across the lawn, a sprinkler lifting
its tired arc and letting it fall. All things
moving to an end. In the loveseat
under the apple tree I open
The Art of Memory and laugh
out loud when I forget the place
I stopped at yesterday. Soon
I'll go in, wake you from your nap
and start our supper, anything
the garden's greens have left to give,
lettuce and chard, that undertaste of
bitterness. We live with who we are and not
what we once wanted. Late August,
its weight on my shoulders, my hand
not on your skin. I turn back
the page and start again,
not sure if I've read
this part before.

NO MUSIC IN IT

The sun takes longer to rise:
it bears a burden it cannot carry.
Darkness lengthens in the day
and inside me
until I walk on stilts of it,
looking down on everything.

I take no pleasure. After dawn
a raven passes overhead.
He takes none either. Measures
daylight's this and this
on noisy wings. Blowing in
a bone flute that has no holes.

BIRTHDAY WITH MY MOTHER

In Swift Current I wake in the cot
in my mother's sewing room, and I am fifty-two.
She pokes her head through the door –
You weren't born yet. Don't get up
till after supper. The exact time
she's not sure of, but I made her miss
the evening meal and she was hungry.

Part of me slips inside her,
behind her eyes now bluer since
the cataracts were peeled away.
How wonderful, after all this time
to be inside my mother
where I grew my bones, my heart.
At eighty-two, she's so small
she hasn't left me any room for sadness.

I'm close to leaving her, late afternoon,
when she walks between the pea vines
in the cracked white sandals she saves
for gardening and the John Deere cap
my father wore, her hair now thin.
Into a tin pail she drops pod after pod,
the sound is heavy rain falling onto cotton.

Two Lake Pelletier perch, their heads
intact, gleam in the kitchen sink

as if Dad has just come back from fishing
and left them for our evening meal.
She'll serve it later than she usually does –
peas, perch floured and fried in butter,
red potatoes in their jackets.

MEASURE

The sun leaning south has a slow drawl,
drawing out the day's vowels,
taking longer to say but still saying it.

It's the end of summer, petals closing up,
the bones in my wrists the first to feel
the possibility of frost.

What I've read and remember pleases me
but has little use – Solzhenitsyn's sister
calling cats the only true Christians

or Aldous Huxley, impatient with the coolness
of Virginia Woolf, her meanness to a friend,
writing in a letter, *She's a jar of ashes.*

I wish I'd saved my father's, sealed some
in an egg timer and used it as a measure,
following the sun's slide across the windowsill,

its slow ease into night. I'm looking more like him,
my face getting thinner, my lips more pinched.
Still, I love the way the sun moves

around *lobelia, anemone, geranium,*
words lasting longer on the warmth
and thickness of its tongue.

BELOW ZERO

The winter boat reaches shore
and skids onto heavy snow. Above it
the sky migrates from east to west.
There is foxfrost on the harbour lantern.
Whoever beached the boat has turned
backwards into wind, white among
the other whiteness. The wildness
invisible. Not even any tracks
from here to there.

LATE AUGUST THRENODY

Two cats in the garden
under different stones.
The slow unravelling

of wind and dahlias
makes a quiet music that moves
with the light low to the ground.

I, too, lay my head
on a cold pillow. Sometimes
it is night, sometimes not.

The dahlias as they dry
and curl in the wind
are what the cats must hear

when all they are is a silence
and then a listening – moonlight
blindly entering a room.

WIND/MIND

Wind presses its forehead against the ground,
against the sky. What a meeting of minds is there!

Wind presses its forehead against the sea,
the chestnut tree, against you walking into morning.

What scree! What desolation!
As if you were standing on a treeless peak

in driving snow, the stars that once were human
wheeling all around you, pitiless and cold.

SMALL GESTURE

Before she moves head down into the dark,
the woman pauses beneath the streetlight,
turns up her collar. Black wool coat.
Now she is a body of pure grief.

From the upstairs window you watch the streetlight
flash her picture, one of several slides
you'll save on the wheel of winter,
this one called

Small Gesture Against the Cold.

BLIZZARD

Walking into wind, I lean into my mother's muskrat coat;
around the cuffs her wristbones have worn away the fur.

If we stood still we'd disappear. There's no up or down,
no houses with their windows lit. The only noise is wind

and what's inside us. When we get home my father
will be there or not. No one ever looks for us.

I could lie down and stay right here where snow is all
that happens, and silence isn't loneliness just cold

not talking. My mother tugs at me and won't let go.
Then stops to find her bearings. In our hoods of stars

we don't know if anyone will understand
the tongue we speak, so far we are from home.

THE END OF THE CENTURY

Under the bridge the dead are gathering.
What happened to the ferryman,
his bag of coins, his pity? In all this traffic
how can they cross these girders of steel
and starlight? One of them hears a creaking.
It is you in your father's rowboat,
newly painted. Your lunch beside you
on the seat, in the bow that singer
who died young. He has spelled you
on this journey but now he begins
in Mandarin the version of Red River
he learned in exile in the fields
far from Beijing. Under the bridge,
hearing him, the dead, too, start singing
We will miss your bright eyes
and sweet smile, in at least
a dozen different tongues.

ACKNOWLEDGEMENTS

The title "Hoping to Fix Up, a Little, This World" is a line from the poet Larry Leavis.

Some of these poems were published in *Grain, Event, The Windsor Review, Descant, Border Crossings, Southern Review, Nimrod, Tieferet, CVII, Prairie Fire,* and the anthology *Poetry International, 7/8.*

My heartfelt appreciation goes to the editor of this collection, Jan Zwicky, for her quick poetic intelligence, to Heather Sangster for her sharp eye, and to Patrick Lane, who always reads my new work before anyone else and who keeps me going. This book would not have been written without the research support of the University of Victoria and without the Saskatchewan Writers Guild's Writer/Artist Colony where I continue to write most of my early drafts.